The Magnificent Light of Morning

Mattie McClane

Myrtle Hedge Press

ISBN: 978-1-7329970-0-4
Library of Congress Control Number: 2021931081

Design and layout by
        Val Sherer, Personalized Publishing Services
Photo 183013408 © Diego Munoz Aviles | Dreamstime.com

To Tim, the man in the yellow boat.

Foreword

On January 6, 2021, democracy was violently assaulted. Rioters, fed lies, invaded the Capital Building where Congress convened to certify the presidential election results. Led by a sitting president, it was an unsuccessful coup. Its infamy is lasting and its perpetrators are not gone.

As an American citizen, the siege was heartbreaking. As a poet, the event called me to a greater appreciation of my craft, because language leans toward the truth. The act of creating a poem requires exactness when choosing words. The poetic process cannot err as the bard assumes the role, the responsibility of witnessing events, ideas, and even objects in society. The mind's eye sees a small thing with four wheels. In the poet's quest for accurate naming, he or she decides if it is a wagon or a cart; it is a wagon, thus the repeated decision-making about word choice results in truth. In times of turmoil, the poet's work becomes necessary and essential.

The 20th Century poet Carl Sandburg said that poetry is "a synthesis of hyacinths and biscuits." His description is seemingly discordant; it does not seem to make sense. Sometimes people say that they don't understand poetry. Poetry is such a close form, meaning the only thing between the wordsmith and paper might be God. It focuses on the human interior, the poet's being. It's proximity to the poet's inner self, not only makes sense, it's impossible to lie.

For that reason, the authoritarian regime often targets poetry because it defies propaganda.

The Magnificent Light of Morning is a synthesis of the public and the private realm, the secular and the sacred. Prompted by Lacanian psychoanalytic theory, it explores time as history, being male, or the Symbolic, and fluidity as female, or the Semiotic. In it, I confront domestic and institutional violence, contrasting these aspects with the calming characteristics of nature.

I thank my husband John, a healer, Dennis Sampson, a poet, and the literary women who have all helped me become a better artist. I'm grateful for my constant God; I believe truth is sacred.

Mattie McClane
Wilmington, NC
February 2, 2021

The Magnificent Light of Morning

"In the shortest sea voyage there is no sense of time. You have been down in the cabin for hours, days, or years. Nobody knows or cares… You do not believe in dry land any more-you are caught in the pendulum itself, and left there, idly swinging."

—Katherine Mansfield

"Water does not resist. Water flows. When you plunge your hand into it, all you feel is a caress. Water is not a solid wall, it will not stop you. But water goes where it wants to go, and nothing in the end can stand against it … Remember that you are half water. If you can't go through an obstacle, go around it. Water does."

–Margaret Atwood

"She looked into the distance, and the
old terror flamed up again for an instant,
then sank again. Edna heard her father's
voice and her sister Margaret's. She
heard the barking of the old dog that was
chained to the sycamore tree. The spurs
of the cavalry officer clanged as he walked
across the porch. There was the hum of bees,
and the musky odor of pinks filled the air."

–Kate Chopin
The Awakening

"War is a man's game … the killing
machine has a gender, and it is male."

–Virginia Woolf
Three Guineas

The Magnificent Light
Of Morning

I

I leave the lake triumphant
old signs present
and cooled
by the clear water July days, nights
the time
is suspended hour-like minutes
every noticed clock
an amazement
How could it be?
We have laughed played until
the air turns gray
from lack
of sunlight night creeps
becomes alive
on the wild shores
animals make
their move undetected

by the resting boaters
perfectly tanned
in preparation
for the work day
office politics
the snub falls away
does not last
because youth
is brilliant
assured
of opportunity offers
before the wing
is constructed across
from an art gallery
with this day there
is hope resilience
what the body and mind gather
from myths

from Ponce de Leon
the fountain searched for
for a lifetime
the white cream removes lines
and long repeated stories
the listener pauses
there is politeness
or indifference
It's hard to tell which
what is true.

I remember a cheap
window covered
with frost cold wet
to the touch on
the inside
where the furnace coughed
the rest

is told in pictures
attempts
to capture
stop time
from ruining afternoons
yellowing
albums bought
in easy installments
to see where
desire began small
simple thoughts
grow become graduate papers
but keep going
like worn shoes
detached
from the leather
its strings
the legs

are strong
have walked
around paths
since beginnings
of distilleries
and billboards.

Time brings the morning.
Where do we go from here?

The golden light escapes
the cloudbank
is calling moments forward
in a white dress
First Communion
another picture
bucking time
stopping

to record
and satisfy grandparents
the grandfather's
one suit reserved
for occasions
where food and drink
are served
to a group
to relatives
to friends
to neighbors
at the capacity appropriate venue
a shell-shocked preacher
is there with cakes
past the expiration
dates free
and loaded
into a Volvo trunk

at the local grocery store.
Time allows him
to tell stories years later
when the mind
shrinks holding
the important
three elements
of the trauma
over and over again
What does
time care anyway?
No, time doesn't tear up
for lost puppies
or any memories
of men with blown faces
from a war
that everyone came
to and left less whole.

No one should
call time father
It is thirty-something
and a born leader
It leads politicians
to rail against
term limits.
they were
just elected
time passes
and they haul out
the old signs, asking
for votes. Time
is a marker. Love
does not matter
to it. It has no intention
of returning
affection.

The Magnificent Light of Morning

Every real lover
knows timing
is always bad
but time changes minutes
in a beloved's presence
the clock
then speeds
to the parting slows
to eternity
when waiting
for reunion.
But don't think it cares
or wants to make life easy
for foolish hearts.

Snow hangs
from the gutters
like rolls

of white paper
on downtown stores
cover sidewalks
the roofs
of cars hidden
and elevated
from whiteness.
The boy is ten
on his way home
from buying dry beans
and coffee. He rests
in the snow,
keeping
his mother's receipt
in a gloved hand.
He becomes aware
of his life
of a heart beating

cheeks stinging
from a windy freeze.
time pauses
It will let him wonder
about his existence.

Time knows the poor
always waiting
anxiously dreaming
for something better.
Time holds a check
on the first
of the month
the mother
giving a watchful eye
when a milk jug
is half empty
with every swallow

because there might
not be money
for schools supplies
picking them out
in make believe
because charity
makes pencils free
binding thoughts
mending ways
of kind persons
or cold government
offers. Time
dampens fantasy hope
when the goods
are all the same
year after year
the child grows
becomes a man

writing on the back
of cereal boxes
the perfect poem.

A 1960s model car
is parked outside
of an educational
testing center
where the night passed
with thoughts
of briefs decisions
the wish for a shower
the fatigue
the brain-drain
after hours of filling
in the blank
sometimes doubt
sometimes ease

the answer
comes quickly
with everything at stake
the test booklet goes
into a wastebasket
then crank the starter
the long drive across
the windy prairie
its long grass
to a large frame duplex
housing three children

The Magnificent Light of Morning

II

Military dreams
every man a hero packed
into amphibious
war machines
above bombers practice
the sky's roar
of engines
in formation
for the next conflict
where soldiers freeze
in the winter
the wished for
discipline
of loners
who confide
in the family dog
and live

with three
headstrong women.

The household
is grieving
is a place
to be avoided
on a wintry trek.
The flag covers
the casket talk overheard
that the family
is bent over
in grief
others
passing by
like horror
like plague
like fever

is in the home
near the train station.

Time knows the rich suits
with cut flowers
on the lapel.
A soloist's voice fills
the theater
front row seats
in a pre-pandemic scene
walls are erected
with words
and not knowing
other possibilities.
The minutes begin ticking
to another place
another season
another harvest

with the silos filled
with grain
that make
fine bourbon
to pass the common
unextraordinary hours
with a portrait
on yard signs
time finally a success.

Let's hear it for patriarchy
Or not.
for bold institutions
military might
ranked men
systematic hierarchies
our fathers
also had fathers

to model
and imitate people
who do not cry
often except in country songs
where they
are considered outlaws.
the car keys thrown
into a field
on a grassy bluff
for punishment
from a drunken man
blame goes out
but cruelty
is not experienced
only the topic
of stories
about boyhood
I have spoken against you

I've been critical
I have let the world
know my story
and have
seldom considered
yours. Time makes
us reflective
when there
is no other recourse
I surrender hurt
to whoever reads books
or imagines children
left behind.

Time knows the middle-class
two income families crowd
into swimming pools
the trees line

subdivisions
two cars
in the driveway
of a two-story house
with a TV
in the living room
watching sports
rooting
for teams
the call
is to stay home
with an elderly dog
and buy groceries
from Walmart ordered
from a phone
that takes portrait photographs
of children playing
at the beach.

The gray thunder booms
and rolls above
the Sargasso Sea
that changes
with every sight
with wind direction
with shifting sands
sometimes smooth
sometimes blue
the water jumps
and bounces
as brown water
as Coke bottle green
is never the same
it never bores
the imagination
I meditate
on its many appearances eternal

body
lasting flow charging
the shore. I feel closer
to a Midwestern home
to a constant God
and a myrtle grove.

The gulls are watchful
Their turning gaze
seems short
mechanical
as they perch
on seven posts
birds eyeing parked cars
their drivers
their passengers
What can they report
in their chatty

language?
Are there love scenes
to ponder
to gossip about
surfers carrying
their boards
with the profound conviction
that nobody drowns?

Fence pickets on the ground
the hurricane
does not spare
the boats
in the marina
cut loose tossing
in the spray trees down
at both ends
of the block.

The sound
of chainsaws greet
the morning
there is triumph
in the air
the sky is blue now
Time passes
into a new day.

III

I wait for the yellow boat
I walk to the point craning
my neck
to the East
a girl looking
for the beloved
the smell
of tobacco
of oil-mixed fuel
in a small V-bottom
cutting through
summer waves rescuing
from boredom
onlookers
who think
my attention
is too young.

I only know
the sharp bends
of the Green River
the thrill
of a motor defying
the current
around
partially sunken logs
causing the water
to swirl
in jagged
liquid lines
while cows graze
on the high ledge banks.
This is the time I want
a channel
so narrow
so full

so fast
that the flow rushes
past exposed
tree roots
into the wider stream.

The deep scar
on the shoulder
a purple heart
for a marine
for a boy
who was on the swim team
in a mill town
and learned
a carpenter's trade
rebuilding flood
damaged homes
not yet put on stilts.

A brother comes home
in a body bag
someone receives
a perfectly
folded flag
put on bookshelves
while the old man
waits for time
to heal misfortune
the survivor
the man
in the yellow boat
is without stories
is without
children moving
to dairy country.

Time is indifferent

not crying until
it meets academia
the historian
the biographer
giving a narrative
to letters
in storage boxes
in libraries
special collections
the work
of lifetimes
with a call number
He would not phone.
He would not answer.
The loves that are
in dreams
and absent spilt
the river

at the bow. Where
do we go
from here
with the water cut in two?
The wake spreads
to the shore
each side
each wave going
its own way
rocking tied vessels
and little water-logged twigs
that rise
that float
that hop
onto ground. They are
freed from the endless bobbing
a monotonous motion
the unrest

in people's hearts
the political divides
that separate
when everyone proclaims
patriotism while
the hatred surges.

It is better to wait for
the yellow boat
even while drunkards sit
on barstools
everyone
is called a nickname
Whiskey Bob
or Indian Charlie
who profess
to the audience
that friends

are like butter
in the sun
unreliable sots
telling stories
by campfires
near the marina
bull frog lore
the night's chorus
until each fall asleep
under a clear sky.

A flock of pelicans
fly over the house
They are back
from plunging
into January's sea.
All creatures
are hungry

near the ocean
the tides
are predictable
I put on readers
to know
the news finding
once again people
who are needy. Yes, I told
you time knows
with the poor
When is the rent due?
The money does
not go far enough
the hunger
is in children
in dignity
the recognition
that one cannot wait

The Magnificent Light of Morning

for lawmakers
to learn compassion
when the world
is political busy
offering lip service
to appear morally engaged.

Test scores come back
the man runs for Justice
of the Peace.
He drives too fast
is ticketed
rebuked
in a local newspaper
and then
tells his wife
that he's leaving her
for better things.

I just wait
for the yellow boat.
It comes to me
on quiet nights
when the stars shine
when the neighbor's
television
is on and can be
seen through
the blinds
I have always
liked getaway
crafts or whatever else
shows the way out
down wild fast rivers
a sharp turn
to the outdoors.

I once lived in a place
without water
three-day schedules
rationing
to hose down
the thirsty grass.
Like clockwork,
the clouds let down
scatter drops
on tennis courts
in the afternoon
the Chinook winds
quickly dry them
while legislators argue
about rights
to the Colorado river.

The long journey
is over mountains
to find
a frigid lake
near backroad shacks
where hermits
make plans
play out sieges
in their minds
and read anti-government leaflets
an only subscription.
Why is the world so mad?
It does not anticipate
any vessel
to free itself
from grievance
the complaints add up
the lost father

The Magnificent Light of Morning

the man on the cross
the doubt-filled Thomas
in a junk strewn
rocky village
on the way to ski resorts.

Time knows the rich
money is speech
drowning
campaign coffers
until every candidate
is sponsored
by a personal
billionaire
who gives up
on multi-million
dollar homes
thousand-acre ranches

extended family
compounds
for power
for influence
for control
money changes
the world, buries
the utterances
of ordinary men
too much
inequality
graciously
acknowledged
accepted
by stockholders
insider trading
for the souls
the hides
the muscles

the respect
of the less fortunate.

Time deals with them
with the threat of the mob.

IV

The shell-shocked preacher
counsels
veterans
post traumatic
stress patients
who have lost limbs
experiencing
phantom pain
the soldiers
who do not sleep
at night for fear
of the sights
the sounds
of battle. Nightmares
are too frequent
the wives are gone
seeking better

calmer nerves
Time knows
the suffering. No day
old bread
can cure what ails
the haunted
the war torn.
Free doughnuts
are all he can bring
while men go
over the hill
looking for the magnificent
light of morning.

Let's hear it for patriarchy
Or not.

He opens a practice

in a country town
then drinks
too much
sits on town councils
noon lunches
with bankers
while he clenches
the woman's breast
in his fist pulling
and twisting it
spitting curses
He leans over
her kicking
his heavy shoes
at her ankle
until it breaks. The
police come and go.
The officers do

not interfere.

I walk to the point looking
for the yellow boat
that cruises down
the river
past cabins
fish tails swirl
making circles
prompting eddies
on a wet fabric
in the stretch
of stream
where poplars'
green leaves
reflect on
the surface
of water going, moving

to the roller dam.

I cannot see it. I cannot see it.
Tomorrow, I'll return.

I will return
and wonder
if there is not enough
testosterone
in the world
for patriarchs
for military men
for would-be autocrats
for those who play
with balls
give concussions
crunch bones
bruise muscles

on a Saturday afternoon.
Time knows
the brute
Darwinian instincts
the toughest
the strongest
who train
who work
to oppress
to dominate
and prey
on weaker creatures.
Time knows
more than
one man
who would
be Lenin willingly
without pity.

V

Women might not count
on the Church.
Gregorian chants
in baritone
the sacred liturgy
the order
of bishops
the Most Holy Father
says she can only read verse
at Mass
is restricted
relegated to the chairs
near the back
of the cathedral
while priests file
in at an installation.
Everyone has a place

The Magnificent Light of Morning

in the hierarchy
not of heaven
but of robed men
who are called
to an exclusive vocation
brothers all.
She is like
the unnamed woman
who met Jesus
on the way
to crucifixion
"Only weep
for yourself
and your children."

Time knows a constant God
who speaks in the calm of water.

I look at a first love
I didn't think
of a scarred shoulder
the white marred skin.
It did not
signify war
or aggression.
It had nothing to do
with hate
no foreign
relation's
failures
only the joy
of a man
who loved the water.

Frost melts
in golden

sunlight
glimmering rays
of morning
release
the frozen
slough.
After due
consideration
second loves
are women
Woolf
Chopin
Naslund
who return
to water
to amniotic
fluids
the wombs

of mothers
embrace
the incessant
rocking
the depth
solid
tight
wholeness
to warm
enclosure
seeking
the healer
above all things.

The healer steps
into the river
is immersed
in baptismal springs

the world hopes
offers prayers
in silence
for a gentler way
a man stands
at the podium
fireworks shoot
into the sky
the father
is pleased
the son renewed
as the people
anticipate
an alternative
to the broken past.

It's the victory of water.
It's the victory of light.